Winds of Change

MAKING TRANSITION

Donald Rumble

Copyright 1986
Destiny Image Publishers
351 North Queen Street
Shippensburg, PA 17257
All Rights Reserved
For Worldwide Distribution
I.S.B.N. 0-914903-12-8

Foreword

"The greatest mistake," wrote A. W. Tozer, "is to resist change." Nonetheless, such resistance appears endemic to human nature. The challenge of change threatens our security and makes us feel vulnerable. Spiritual growth, however, requires constant change both in individuals and in congregations, and this is the central theme of Don Rumble's book.

The Apostle Paul wrote, "But we all, with open face beholding in a glass the glory of the Lord, are changed into the same image from glory to glory, even as by the Spirit of the Lord" (2 Cor. 3:18). What a different point of view concerning change this presents to the believer—God changing His children from *glory* to *glory*.

This excellent booklet by Don Rumble declares the glory of change. It carries a prophetic anointing from the heart of God.

As I read the three pithy chapters of *Winds of Change,* I was challenged to face the areas in my life where I have been resisting God's work of transition and I discovered that I have not been as open to God's workmanship as I previously believed.

Don shows us that God wants to bring us out of mind-sets and belief systems based exclusively on past experiences so He can continually bring us into His "newness of life." The teaching of this booklet, therefore, has applications for our individual lives as well as for our corporate worship. It calls us to move on *with God* as He continues to prepare us for that wonderful day when "the earth shall be filled with the knowledge of the glory of the Lord, as the waters cover the sea" (Hab. 2:14).

A whole new realm of spiritual life and truth awaits all who will be truly open to God's moving in our midst. A glorious, fresh outpouring of God's Spirit is on the way! This tidal wave of truth will sweep us along to higher plateaus of spiritual life if we will but be open to God's changing power. As you read this book, new openness will come to you.

The familiar chorus reveals God's expectations for you and me:

> *From glory to glory He's changing me,*
> * changing me.*
> *His likeness and image to perfect in me,*
> *The love of God shown to the world.*
> *For He's changing, He's changing me,*
> *From earthly things to the heavenly,*
> *His likeness and image to perfect in me,*
> *The love of God shown to the world.*

It is my sincere conviction that your reading of *Winds of Change* will permit God to do a new work in your heart and life. Isn't that exciting?

May God continue to inspire Don Rumble to produce works of lasting significance for the Body of Christ.

Lloyd B. Hildebrand
Oxford, New Jersey

Contents

Preface

And this is eternal life, that *they may know Thee,* the only true God, and Jesus Christ whom Thou hast sent. (John 17:3, italics mine)

The greatest privilege ever given to man has been offered to us! The King of the universe has granted us an audience!

Most of us have never been invited to visit the head of a country. The experience of sitting with royalty or with well-known political leaders is a dream. Yet, the One who invites us surpasses them all in glory and beauty!

He is the personification of wisdom. In righteousness and justice, His way is perfect. He is altogether lovely and greatly to be desired. What a joy He is! All of life takes on new meaning in His presence. The most beautiful things ever created pale in comparison to Him. Absolute commitment to Him becomes the obvious response when one stands before Him. He is life itself.

Unfortunately, many of God's people squander this great gift of eternal life. They seem to believe that knowing Him is either a one-time experience (e.g. at repentance: "Oh, yes, I know the Lord. I met Him two years ago."), or it will only be meaningly fulfilled at His return. But Jesus said:

. . . *I came that they might have life, and might have it abundantly. (John 10:10)*

Now is the time to experience eternal life—today, tomorrow and forever!

Now is 'the acceptable time,' behold, now is 'the day of salvation . . . .' " (2 Cor. 6:2)

It is God's intention that we know Him more intimately each day of our lives. The abundant life He has promised is not related to material goods and money (e.g. the American dream), rather it is measured in terms of our relationship with Him!

We must not put off to the future, or relegate to the past, what God intends for the present. Certainly our knowledge of Him at the time of His return will be great for then we shall see Him face to face. However, we are called to live in union with Him today; we are to be a people of life—now! Indeed, His life is what makes us unique in the world.

The Fragrance

But thanks be to God, who always leads us in His triumph in Christ, and manifests through us the sweet aroma of the knowledge of Him in every place, for we are a fragrance of Christ to God among those who are being saved and among those who are perishing; to the one an aroma from death to death, to the other an aroma from life to life. And who is adequate for these things? (2 Cor. 2:14-16)

When Christians dedicate themselves to knowing the Lord in an intimate way, a fragrance will arise in their lives. To God, it is the sweet fragrance of His Son! To others, it can be an aroma leading either to life or to death, depending on the condition of their hearts. But who is adequate for such a ministry? How does one start exuding the fragrance of Christ? Can it be "turned on" at will? Obviously not. In fact, what Paul is discussing here is beyond human resources. Either this fragrance is in our lives, or it is not! To the degree we give ourselves to Him, it is there. To the degree we fail to do so, it is not. Sadly, the sweet aroma of the knowledge of Christ is not found, as it ought to be, in the Church. The reason is simple. We fail to pay the price of spending time in His presence! So many other things "need" to be done. Ministry to others demands much of our time. Our priorities are wrong.

We must face this issue. The supernatural unveiling of Christ in and through us is beyond our ability to control! We simply can not turn it on or off. We must spend time with Him so that He can unveil himself to us. There, in His presence, a transformation takes place within us, and a sweet aroma begins to permeate our hearts. Knowledge can be *taught;* this fragrance must be *caught!* It is a supernatural event. As a consequence, our lives begin to give forth that sweet aroma everywhere we go. Thus it is *God* who is manifesting through us the "flavor" of His Son; it is *not* our striving to be like Jesus. How He longs to be unveiled in us! Thus, He continually draws us to himself, wooing us to become more a people of His presence.

What does this have to do with transition? It is the heart of it! We must spend time in His presence if we are to move with Him in the fulfillment of His plan for this age.

1
Knowing God's Ways

Someone has said, "Constant change is here to stay." I believe this statement aptly describes life in the Kingdom of God. He is ever leading us onward. When Jesus says, "Follow me," to His people, the implication is clear. His intention is not to preserve the status quo in our lives, but to bring us into the fulfillment of God's purposes.

There was a joy set before Jesus almost 2,000 years ago. He pressed forward and paid an awful price to see it realized. It is our privilege to join with Him today as He continues moving toward His ultimate goal: to conform us into His likeness.

Building in an Earthquake

The Lord said that Jeremiah was called:

To pluck up and to break down, to destroy and to overthrow, to build and to plant . . . . (Jer. 1:10)

I used to interpret this as follows: "First you break down and destroy, *then* you will build and plant." However, the shaking and building happen simultaneously. God is the only One I know of who builds in an earthquake! It is in the *midst* of shaking that God exposes our hearts and shows us our need for Him and for one

1

another. He wants us to "lay hold" of Him *in* our trying circumstances and to share with others out of what He builds in us. The building of character takes place while we are *in* the refining process. The belief that we must first get all imperfections out of the way before God will use us can hinder us; it causes us to focus more on our defects than on looking to Him. Indeed, it is in our weaknesses that His presence and strength become more real to us.

What a joy it is to know that He loves us and receives our service at our present level of growth. However, He also intends for us to grow up!

Electric Worship

In 1971 the Lord spoke very clearly to me. After several years of backsliding I had just rededicated my life to Him. As I was reading the Scriptures, Psalm 37:4 came alive to me:

Delight yourself in the Lord; and He will give you the desires of your heart.

Immediately I knew what He meant to give me. During the past several years I had been playing at night clubs with various hard rock bands. Now that I was back in right relationship with Him, I "just knew" He wanted me to start a "Jesus rock" group. "Oh, boy," I thought, "electric worship!" However, the more I tried, the fulfillment of my dream seemed further away. As I practiced with different brothers, I realized there was a distinct lack of anointing on the music we played. I tried various combinations of musicians, but nothing worked. I did not know what to do. I knew I had heard from God. What was wrong? Finally, I had to lay the vision down.

The answer was in the heart of God; if I was going to find it, I would have to stay close to Him. As I walked with the Lord over the next couple of years, He began to open doors for me to teach the Scriptures. I found myself sharing in coffee houses, churches, and youth meetings. One night, as I was speaking to a group of young people, He said something to me I have never forgotten: *"Son, this ministry is the desire of your heart; the other was the desire of your soul."* I suddenly realized I had not known my own heart!

Fulfillment is never found in doing what we *want*; it is found in our *obedience*. We can not discern the depths of our own hearts; but He who made us can. As we search His Word and follow Him, we will come to know Him better and our own hearts as well. Real joy comes by doing what He asks. Gradually it will dawn on us that *His* way really is best, and that He has our own best interests at heart. Wholeness and fulfillment are found in His will for our lives.

Thou wilt make known to me the path of life; in thy presence is fulness of joy . . . . (Ps. 16:11)

We make successful transitions in the purposes of God as we walk in obedience *to Him.*

Faithfulness to God

God seeks for us to become a faithful people. The generation that did not enter the Promised Land was:

A stubborn and rebellious generation that did not prepare its heart, and whose spirit was not faithful to God. (Ps. 78:8, emphasis mine)

In order to make a successful transition into new dimensions of the purposes of God, we must prepare our hearts to be faithful to what He reveals to us. God

3

sends His prophetic word to foretell of things to come and calls us to prepare accordingly. Many hear His words, but few make the transition. One reason some fail is because it is easier to be *faithful to a task* the Lord gave us in the *past* than to be faithful to hear and obey Him *now*. God assigns special tasks for a season. Often they are used to train us for greater responsibility. The time comes, however, when He wants us to move into a new sphere of service. If what we have been doing has become the focus of our lives rather than hearing the Lord, we will be left behind. What is worse—we may not even know it! Those who are faithful *to Him* are the ones who will make the transition. The fruitfulness and dimensions of our service will grow only as we grow in our knowledge of *Him*.

Also, let us never forget in serving that we are servants of *the Lord*. Servants must be quick to respond to their master's new command. Some hear a valid word from God and become involved in a work that was God's will for them at the time. Later, as God begins to move with a new emphasis, they remain active in what God *had said* yesterday rather than what He *is saying* today.

One way to discern if we are in God's present emphasis is to observe what foundation our work rests on. When *God* is doing something, it requires no support other than himself. Human strategies, striving, and programs with many requests for money to support a ministry are generally indications that men are trying to keep something alive which is secondary to the purposes of God.

Hidden Truth

I often marvel at the way God accomplishes His will. Sometimes it almost seems His intention is to confuse those who study the Scriptures! Consider the Messianic promise in Zechariah 9:9-10:

Rejoice greatly, O daughter of Zion . . . ! Behold, your king is coming to you; He is just and endowed with salvation . . . and mounted on a donkey . . . and I will cut off the chariot from Ephraim, and the horse from Jerusalem; and the bow of war will be cut off. And He will speak peace to the nations; and His dominion will be from sea to sea, and from the River to ends of the earth.

After reading this passage, I understood why Jewish people had the expectations they did concerning their Messiah. When He came, they expected Him to ride into town, smash all weapons of war, and establish a worldwide kingdom characterized by peace and harmony. Clearly, parts of these verses have not yet been fulfilled. As a matter of fact, it seems as though there is a 2,000-year interval between verses nine and ten! The abolition of weapons of war and the establishment of world peace will only be fully realized when Jesus returns. Until then, there will be wars and rumors of wars. Jesus has fulfilled part of this passage, but certainly not all of it—yet.

Why did the Lord not mention that there was a 2000-year interval between verses nine and ten? It would have made it easier for people to understand His plan. This raises the question, "Does God give insight concerning His intentions to everyone?" I do not think so. He hides himself and His ways *so that they may only be revealed to those who seek Him!*

I doubt if Zechariah himself understood the consequences of his prophetic word. He probably thought it meant that the Messiah would come and immediately set up a visible worldwide kingdom, removing war from the earth. And he would have been incorrect!

Those who prophesy must be careful to bring only the word God gives them. Adding an interpretation to what God has said is to introduce their opinion. A distinction must be made between revelation and interpretation. Many times when God fulfills what He has said, *all* are surprised at how He accomplishes it, *including the prophets who predicted it!*

When the Jewish people read this passage in Zechariah concerning the Messiah's coming, they had an accurate knowledge of the original language in which it was written. Many studied the book of Zechariah and listened to teachers who had devoted their lives to understanding the Scriptures. They probably were aware that verses should not be taken "out of context" but be seen as integral parts of the whole picture. Yet, with all these positive elements of their study of the Bible, it was generally those who were *most* involved in Scripture study who did not believe Jesus to be their Messiah!

God hides truths from the wise and intelligent and reveals them to babes (Matt. 11:25). *It is those who walk in childlike humility with their heavenly Father who will grasp the secrets of His heart. If, in addition to our "correct" methods of Bible study and interpretation, we do not walk close to Him as little children, we will misunderstand and misinterpret His activity on the earth!*

Knowing His Ways

Our God is awesome! He is mighty, magnificent, and is greatly to be feared! Our one great quest in this life is to know Him and His ways:

This is eternal life, that they may know Thee, the only true God, and Jesus Christ whom Thou hast sent. (John 17:3)

The Scriptures say:

He made known His ways to Moses, His acts to the sons of Israel. (Ps. 103:7)

We are to give ourselves wholeheartedly to knowing Him and His ways. Knowing about His acts is good, but knowing His heart and *why* He acts is much greater. Most of us can recall some recent acts of God. We have seen people healed, saved and delivered. We have seen marriages restored. Seeing this activity brings us great joy. But do we walk close enough to Him to know His heart and have insight concerning how He feels? When we speak His words, do we only speak the correct words or do we also speak them out of a heart that expresses His heart? Jesus said:

Whatever the Father does, these things the Son also does in like manner. (John 5:19, emphasis mine)

The things I speak, I speak just as the Father has told Me. (John 12:50, emphasis mine)

We must learn His ways! There will come a day when:

Many nations will come and say, 'Come and let us go . . . to the house of the God of Jacob, that He may teach us about His ways . . .' (Mic. 4:2)

If people are coming to God's house to know His ways, we had better spend time learning them!

God's Unfathomable Ways

How unsearchable are His judgments and unfathomable His ways! (Rom. 11:33)

7

A fathom is a measure of *depth*. Paul states that God's ways are so deep they cannot be measured. This means I could spend my whole life endeavoring to understand the depth of His ways and only "scratch the surface"! Also, the Lord expresses it this way:

As the heavens are higher than the earth, so are My ways higher than your ways . . . . (Isa. 55:9)

Here He indicates the *height* of His ways. How high are the heavens? Has anyone ever discovered their vastness? The Lord says that to learn His ways is a lifetime task; even then, we will have only begun. Moses, who knew God's ways, only "scratched the surface." Paul, who knew the Lord for many years, still had one supreme quest in his life: he wanted to know Him more intimately:

More than that, I count all things to be loss in view of the surpassing value of knowing Christ Jesus my Lord . . . that I may know Him . . . . (Phil. 3:8,10, emphasis mine)

We know Him; and yet how little we know Him! We know His ways, but we have so much more to learn! As little children, we must continually come to our Father with open, humble and teachable hearts, for we are called to know what is beyond our human capacity of knowledge!

To know the love of Christ which surpasses knowledge . . . . (Eph. 3:19, emphasis mine)

Truly our God is awesome!

Surprise!

Since we are children with so much to learn, it is foolish to think that our predictions of what God will do next are a final word or the total picture. The truth is that God continually surprises us by what He does in our midst. Many times I have thought to myself, "I would not have done it that way." I have frequently found God extending more mercy than I would have in certain situations. I have also seen Him deal severely in people's lives and keep the pressure on long after I thought He ought to ease up! God knows the hearts of His people better than anyone and, therefore, He knows just what is needed to bring us to maturity. God loves "in the extreme," and He judges "in the extreme."

I have often thought that Stephen, whose martyrdom is recorded in Acts 7, would have been an effective apostle for the Lord. He operated in tremendous wisdom, authority and power; yet he was humble enough to wait on tables. Saul of Tarsus, on the other hand, probably would not have been on *anyone's* list of likely candidates for apostleship (except the Lord's!). Stephen was killed and Saul was converted. What a contrast to the way we would have chosen!

Consider, too, that James was slain and Peter was rescued (Acts 12:1-11). While Peter was in prison, the Scriptures say:

Prayer for him was being made fervently by the church to God. (Acts 12:5)

I imagine the church prayed fervently on behalf of James, too; nevertheless, God's ways are not our ways! It seems that if anybody was guaranteed a long, effective life and ministry, it should have been James. He was one of the three who saw Jesus transfigured (Matt. 17:1,2)! He was invited by the Lord to watch and pray with Him at the most crucial time in His earthly ministry (Matt. 26:36-38). James was close to the Lord; yet Jesus saw fit to take him home early. Peter, on the other hand, was dramatically rescued by an angel. Even though the saints were praying for his release, they were amazed when he arrived at their prayer meeting. What an awesome God we serve! With all our insight concerning things to come, much that happens continues to surprise us, and causes us to declare He is indeed a mighty God! Worship arises from those who see Him to be much more than they had expected.

The Next Wave

God is doing a new thing today! A "new wave" of His presence and power is here. As I write this, there are indications we are in the beginning stages of a fresh visitation from heaven! This present thrust of the Holy Spirit will not be identical to the last one. It will not be "more of the same, only bigger." There are surprises in store for us!

Take heed therefore, so that the thing spoken of in the Prophets may not come upon you: 'Behold, you scoffers, and marvel, and perish (lit., to disappear); for I am accomplishing a work in your days, a work which you will never believe, though someone should describe it to you.' (Acts 13:40-41)

Witnesses describe what they have seen. When Jesus said we are to be His witnesses, His intent is that we not only observe and describe what He has done, but also what He *is doing!* To be His witnesses, we must be a prophetic people! To speak only of what Jesus did historically is to give only part of the message. Many Christians are sitting idly by, awaiting the rapture, and they do not comprehend the present activities of Jesus on earth. How then can they speak accurately on His behalf?

When Paul spoke the above words, recorded in Acts 13, he was describing what was then the present thrust of the Holy Spirit to those who were identified with the previous move of God. Messiah had come, died, arose, ascended and poured out the Holy Spirit on His followers. Ambassadors were now going about describing this new thing God was doing. And Paul had a warning for his listeners. If their hearts were not right before God (scoffers), they would marvel at what they saw, but they would *disappear* from the scene. They would not make the transition!

Paul's quotation was taken from what God had spoken to the prophet Habakkuk. The "next wave" in Habakkuk's day was one of judgment. God was bringing the Babylonians upon His people as the rod of His discipline. In effect, the Lord told the prophet that even if He himself was to describe to him what was coming, Habakkuk would not have believed it! Sure enough, in chapter one we find Habakkuk questioning how God could do such a thing. Citing how the Babylonians were more wicked than the Jews, he questioned the wisdom of God in using such people to effect His judgments. It is good to keep in mind that Habakkuk, who had such a hard time embracing what God was about to do, was not a shallow, carnal individual. He was one who stood in the position of a prophet in Israel. He knew the Lord well and had heard His voice clearly. Thus, no matter how mature one is, there is the ever-present need to be humble, broken and teachable. Pride always disqualifies us. Those who proudly state they know what God is about to do, will most probably "miss it." Herein lies the danger: those who have received the most light are more likely to miss God if their hearts are not tender before Him.

The Scriptures say knowledge puffs up but love builds up (1 Cor. 8:1). When something is puffed up, it looks greater than it really is (e.g. size without substance). How easy it is to think of someone (or ourselves) as being mighty in God because of insight in the Scriptures. One may have many revelations of truth yet not walk in them. There is a vast difference between knowing what we should do, and doing it! I may know that God wants me to be patient; but do I bear the fruit of patience? Knowing the truth of overcoming in Christ does not mean I am an overcomer. Knowledge is not the essence of the Kingdom, whereas the character of God (love) is.

Satan tempts us to put our trust more in what we know than in Him who reveals truth. On the other hand, the Lord seeks to develop in us a continual dependence upon Him. *Increased revelation without a corresponding degree of brokenness is dangerous.*

When we respond in humility to God's word, it will work change in us. However, if we are hearers and not doers, we will grow arrogant (1 Cor. 8:1).

Thinking ourselves to be more than we are, we become deceived. Deception is not primarily a fault of the mind, but of heart attitude. We may be accurate in doctrine, and yet be deceived.

For if anyone thinks he is something when he is nothing, he deceives himself. (Gal. 6:3)

We might know what is to come yet not know the condition of our own hearts. The Pharisees had many correct doctrines, but they were far from God. They failed to make the transition into God's purposes for their day.

Even though it was difficult for him to make the adjustment and embrace what God was about to do, Habakkuk made this statement at the end of his prophetic writings:

I must wait quietly for the day of distress, for the people to arise who will invade us. Though the fig tree should not blossom, and there be no fruit on the vines . . . yet I will exult in the Lord, I will rejoice in the God of my salvation. (Hab. 3:16-18)

In effect, he said that even if there was total desolation, he would rejoice in the Lord. He was a man ready to make the transition. For Habakkuk, the Lord was enough; he would be faithful to Him.

Transition in the Local Church

We all find ourselves in local assemblies that have imperfections. At the same time, we desire to move on in God's purposes, and we want those around us to do so as well. Sometimes these imperfections can be very frustrating. There is a temptation to search for the perfect church. However, we will never find one. God seeks to teach us how to stand and minister His life in less-than-perfect situations and how to grow in maturity.

It is not difficult to find imperfections in the church because flaws in others are often more obvious to us than our own. How easy it is to think, "If only those around me were more spiritual, then I could be all God wants me to be." This comes from a spiritual malady described by some as, "The If Onlies." It is expressed by such statements as, "If only our elders could preach better," or "If only my husband was more sensitive to the Spirit," or, "If only the musicians could sing better," etc. Adam evidenced this when confronted by God in the Garden of Eden.

'The woman whom Thou gavest to be with me, she gave me from the tree, and I ate.' (Gen. 3:12)

The implication was that if only God had given him a better wife, he would have overcome. In other words, it was really God's fault! There are many excuses we can come up with as to why we fail to express God's life in our particular circumstances. If we excuse our failures, we imply that the basis of victorious living is the situations of life rather than the Lord Jesus. This is a wrong foundation.

We must not justify our stumbling. God wants us to stand and minister His life in the midst of an imperfect church and in times of personal distress. He allows us to see faults in others so we can intercede for them and redeem the situation through our words and actions.

It is one thing to *start* influencing others toward greater godliness; it is another to *persist* in the work He has given us to do. Endurance is necessary for us to overcome our circumstances and move on in God's purposes. Jesus said:

The one who endures to the end, he shall be saved . . . . (Matt. 24:13)

What is the key to endurance (e.g. a consistent life style)? First of all, our motive must be God's will for us—and that alone. We do not minister for recognition; we minister because He desires it. We live where we do, drive the car we do, attend the church we are involved with, work at our place of employment, etc. all for one reason. It is His will! Our desire is simply to be and do what He wants. To please Him is the driving force of our lives.

*We have as our ambition, . . . to be pleasing to Him.
(2 Cor. 5:9)*

No other motivation will sustain us when the inevitable trials come.

If our motive is to establish New Testament Christianity in the local church God has related us to, we will eventually be frustrated with the imperfections of those around us. It is so easy to see how others fall short; how they hinder what God is doing. It is not so easy to consistently cover these imperfections with life and wisdom from a servant's attitude.

Recently, I was speaking in a church that had some problems. There were several factions. Some had wrong heart attitudes, and others were content with the condition of the fellowship. One dear sister came up to me and began to describe the situation correctly. I was impressed with her accuracy. I was also conscious that many times those with accurate discernment can often do tremendous damage in the church. Diagnosing the problem is often much easier than effecting the cure!

As I talked with this sister, I told her she had three choices:

1. Be part of the problem (e.g. contribute to gossip, backbiting, grumbling, etc.) This was obviously not correct.
2. Leave the fellowship. God could lead in this direction.
3. Be part of God's solution. Those who choose this option learn to minister God's life in the midst of imperfection. This is how leaders are developed. People will follow those who have the life of God.

The sister was shown the need so that she could pray for the church and be an example of servanthood.

We must "wash people's feet" with the truth, not attack them with it. Jesus "washed the feet" of the disciples for three years while He patiently taught and explained the purposes of God to them. When He girded himself with a towel at the Last Supper, what He was about to do was but an extension of what He had been doing all along. Those who would make foot washing a part of church liturgy but who do not serve the saints with truth, misunderstand the whole point of John 13.

The church today is in transition. There is a need for men and women to emerge in local assemblies with the wisdom of God in their mouths. Those who find Him to be their strength in the midst of difficult circumstances will have direction and vision for those around them. When He is the center of our motivation, our lives become an offering unto Him. The imperfections we see around us can not alter our walk; they are not what motivates us. Endurance is established within us. Patience has her perfect work when Christ is central in our lives.

In order for the Church to make the transition and move on in the purposes of God, Jesus must become central in the lives of each individual member. Without this understanding, we will be tempted to withdraw from those who do not meet our "standards," and to gather together with only those with whom we are comfortable. Jesus loves *all* of His people. He longs for His whole body to come to full maturity. If we want to contribute to His purpose in these days, we can not be sectarian. We must be willing to serve *all* of His people if we are to serve Him.

Enjoying the Way

Jesus said He is the way. What does that mean? I believe we will always be in transition until He returns. We can get off the train any time we choose to do so. If we are to go on with Him, however, we must know Him as God's way. We are a people on the way to something. We must not be so concerned with where we are going that we forget to enjoy the way! The saints were not called "the people of the realized goal" in the Scriptures. They were known as those of "the way." God gives glimpses of where we are going so we can overcome *on the way,* and not be overly preoccupied with the goal. Goal-oriented Christianity can be very damaging. For example, it is possible to minister "New Testament Christianity" and hurt people in the process of trying to implement our vision of the local church. It is possible to talk of heaven and sit idly by waiting for the Rapture. "The way" is very important to God. The end does not justify the means. *How* we get where we are going is a key issue. It is good to have godly goals; but it is vital that we allow *God* to bring us into the fulfillment of them. We who have caught a glimpse of where He is going can be very destructive if we are not careful about how we minister to others. In seeking to implement our vision, we can hurt those who do not respond as we think they ought to respond. Knowing Jesus as the way means we trust that *He* will bring to pass what He has promised. He is the way to His goals. Let us press on *in Him,* knowing that His zeal for God's house far surpasses our own.

2

Where Do I Belong?

The Lord first spoke to me about my willingness (or lack of it) to walk as a single man before Him in 1972. While driving home from a friend's house, I was reminding Him of how my friends were getting married, having babies, buying houses, etc. I was thinking, "What are your plans for my life, Lord? Where is she?"

He said something like this, *"Son, I want you willing to be single for the rest of your life."*

I thought, "That isn't really you, is it, Lord?" I have often shared with my friends that He did not command me to remain single for the rest of my life, rather He wanted me to be willing to be so. Recently I have realized that if I really am willing, it does not matter whether I marry or not. Now, instead of differentiating between being single and being willing, I am enjoying the truth of embracing His will. What the future holds for me is in His hands.

Jesus must be central in our lives; everything is to revolve around Him. He will adjust us in those areas where He is not first in our priorities. Individually and corporately, the desire to please Him must be our motive (2 Cor. 5:9). Divine order in the Church can not be achieved apart from this truth. Order is not an external system that governs the actions of God's people; rather it expresses their relationship under His government. It develops organically from life union with

Him. Order exists when He has His way; He is Lord! The local church is where God's people are brought into harmony with one another as they submit to Him. Each of us has a unique place and function to fulfill in His Church.

Defining the Problem

The Church is to be apostolic. Each member is to be actively involved in body life within a unique sphere of responsibility.

But we will not boast beyond our measure, but within the measure of the sphere which God apportioned to us as a measure, to reach even as far as you. (2 Cor. 10:13)

God apportions a sphere of responsibility to each one of us. He knows exactly how much grace we need. He knows what we are able to handle and what we are not. He does not give us more than we can bear. To say, "I do not have the time to do what God wants me to do," indicates either a lack of knowledge concerning what His will is or a lack in appropriating the time He has given. He always provides sufficient grace, time, anointing, etc., to accomplish what He wants done. Remember, His yoke is easy and His burden is light! When such a discrepancy arises, the cause is usually one of the following:

1. We fail to avail ourselves of His supply (i.e., not seeing the grace He has already given for the task at hand, not wisely using the time He has given, etc.)

2. We attempt to do something other than what He has given us to do. If one is called to be a pastor in Cleveland, he will not do well as an evangelist in Afghanistan. Being stirred in one's emotions to go into other lands is not enough to sustain one there. If God

has sent us He will sustain us. Needs alone are not a sufficient reason to go. Many have gone to the mission field, and suffered marital and emotional breakdowns because they went beyond the sphere of God's grace. On the other hand, staying in Cleveland can be just as disastrous if God wants us on the other side of the earth!

3. Mixture. *Part* of what we do is God's will and part is ours. Many saints experience this dilemma. They sense grace and anointing for some of their burden. Yet, there is lack of fruitfulness in other activities and the result is an inner striving and frustration.

The wisdom from above is . . . peaceable, gentle . . . full of good fruits. (James 3:17)

Finding Our Sphere

How does one find his sphere in the Kingdom? The answer to this question can not be found simply through teaching. God's will is always discovered on our knees! However, I would like to share a few insights from experience that can help with this question.

When we first came into God's kingdom, our sphere was not very large. In fact, we were not even concerned about spheres. All we knew was that we loved God and wanted to worship and obey Him. There was no pressure on us to do great things for God. We were spiritual babes; we knew it, but we wanted to learn. However, when Christians are zealous, their desire to mature often produces strange behavior. Babes in the Lord often lose sight of their youthfulness and, in trying to act mature, they can wind up carrying a sense of "responsibility" in ministry that is not God-given. Trying to grow up "too fast" will often produce frustration in them and also bring pain to those around them. While we are to press on toward maturity, we must also be realistic about where we are in God at our present stage of growth (Phil. 3:14,16).

Probably nothing causes strange behavior in Christians more than putting a title next to their names. I used to think, "If only I was an elder, then I would know what to do." I thought definition for my life would come from having a "job description" applied to my ministry. In fact, I had the process backwards. God wants us to walk in the Spirit and let others recognize what we are in God. In time, the word "elder" did become relevant to my ministry.

I remember when hands were laid on me for eldership, I immediately was confronted with a problem. I thought, "Now that I am an elder, I had better act a little holier. After all, now I am a 'man of God'!" I began to behave in a manner I thought was appropriate for an elder. Thank God that while others might have been impressed, the Lord was not. He said something to my spirit that really helped: *"Son, don't try to be what you think others want you to be; just be yourself."* Praise the Lord for His patience and understanding.

If we look back to our childhood years in the Kingdom, we will notice how very easily and naturally God began to establish our spheres. One by one, He began to put people into our lives. We found ourselves enjoying the company of certain ones, and friendships were formed. Friendships and the life flow of God cannot be established by legislation; it must happen organically. I am close to certain brethren, not because I *have* to be, but because it fits! It is right! There is life in it for both them and me.

As an elder, I do believe in seeing young believers

"plugged in" to other more mature Christians in the local church as soon as possible. However, I must be certain that in my zeal for proper order I do not disrupt what the Lord wants done. Unfortunately, mistakes have been made in this area, and the results have seen arm bones "plugged in" to hip sockets! This is painful for all concerned. Builders must cooperate with His life, not supplant it!

A key insight comes to us from Paul's letter to the Ephesians:

The whole body, being fitted and held together by that which every joint supplies . . . (Eph. 4:16)

The members of Christ's body are not held together by law or orders from the leadership. People are bonded to each other in commitment when the joint between them supplies life! A joint is simply that which exists between two members. The word "joint" speaks to us of relationship. When the relationship between another and me supplies life to both of us, it is obvious we belong in each other's lives. However, I will still need discernment and wisdom to understand the degree of involvement that is appropriate.

Two years ago, when several of the home groups in our fellowship were having difficulty, we elders were confronted with the problem of restructuring them. The three groups of concern were in close proximity to each other and each was experiencing a distinct lack of life in their midst. Rather than simply try to reorder things ourselves, the eldership felt God would give wisdom to His people as each one sought His face. (Godly oversight does not involve control over people's lives; and neither does it encourage anarchy.) The home groups were closed down and all the people were brought together for Bible study for a few months and given instruction on foundational topics. All were encouraged to seek the Lord's will concerning His place for them in His body. Over time, different ones came to us expressing a desire to meet again in small groups. Meanwhile, the Lord impressed the eldership with the homes where the new groups would meet, and what men should oversee them. These were men who were committed to us and the vision God had given for the church. We announced the names of leaders and the homes in which the meetings would take place. We then continued the study for several more weeks, encouraging the people to keep praying for personal direction. When the time came to start the small groups again, we were pleasantly surprised to learn afresh that Jesus knows how to build His church! He spoke to each one concerning where they belonged. There was an ideal breakdown in numbers in each home, and there was a good distribution of minstrels for music. Today those meetings are flourishing.

There is a place for each of us in His house, and it fits! He knows how to place us together with the people we need in our lives.

God has placed the members, each one of them, in the body, just as He desired. (1 Cor. 12:18)

Good relationship requires that life flows in both directions between parties. Love is a "two-way street." People who always need input but do not have life to give in return can be a tremendous drain. The remedy is not more counsel. They must be taught how to stand in the Lord's life and, in turn, learn how to minister that life to others. Those who counsel should themselves look for life in the counseling relationships they are involved in. In this way, they can avoid becoming simply one who has answers for others but become members more closely knit to those to whom they minister.

Two Prevalent Problems

Each one of us will stand before the Lord one day and give an account of how we handled the sphere of responsibility He gave us. In that hour we will not be able to blame others for our lack of stewardship. Yet, everywhere I go in the Church I see spheres of responsibility being defined, not so much by what God is saying, but by: 1) the needs of people and 2) the structure of the local church. Neither of these should dictate our sphere of responsibility. Only God is to do that.

1. *Needs:* We are not to be calloused to needs around us. Jesus wept at the suffering and disease He saw afflicting people around Him. However, need did not determine what He was to do. His Father guided Him, and specific needs were met. If we let the needs of others dictate what we are to do, we will be overwhelmed! We must trust that Jesus is able to answer our prayers and the prayers of those who are afflicted. He really does care for each one of us. What are our options? a) He may want us to minister to the need at hand, b) He may want to do it sovereignly himself, c) He may want us to pray that He would raise up one to meet the need.

In any event, our prayer is, "O Lord, what is your will for me in this? Above all else I want to do your will!" The reason there are so many overworked men in Christian leadership is that it is hard to say no. In the gospels we see that Jesus often turned away from needs. Indeed, to understand this is a part of the training of God's sons! Will they hear the guiding voice of the Father, even above the cries of hurting people around them?

How many times did Jesus turn away from needs during the years previous to His baptism? Obviously He saw the many who were crippled, blind and demon-possessed. Despite many such needs, His first miracle was to turn water into wine at a wedding in Cana (John 2:11). For approximately thirty years, He did no miracles. I wonder what it was like for Him to be confined to a carpenter shop seeing these needs? How many times did He have to turn away with tears in His eyes from a lame child or blind beggar as He walked under the discipline of His Father? As He fashioned yokes for the oxen of local farmers, I am sure He often contemplated the Father's yoke upon His own life. He wore that yoke faithfully, and at His baptism, He heard His Father say,

. . . 'This is My beloved Son, in whom I am well-pleased.' (Matt. 3:17)

No other had worn the yoke of God like this One. Jesus walked in such union with His Father that it became such a part of His life that He exhorted others:

Take My yoke upon you, and learn of Me, . . . (Matt. 11:29)

The focus of the Scriptures is for men to know God, to walk with Him faithfully, and to become like Him in character. The issue is not what we can do for God. Rather, it is the way we walk in step with Him, learning His ways, hearing His voice, and doing His will.

Jesus spent approximately ten times as long under the discipline of restraint *from* ministry as He did under the discipline of restraint *in* ministry. Each was extremely important.

How many times did Jesus pass by the lame man at the temple gate called Beautiful? We see Him healing people inside the temple (Matt. 21:14), and yet this particular man's needs were not addressed. He had been lame all his life, and was brought to the gate everyday (Acts 3:2). Could it be that Jesus had not noticed him? Or, could it be that Jesus had an intuitive sense in His heart that the Father intended to minister to this need at another time through other vessels? Jesus faithfully gave himself to the task of doing what His Father wanted Him to do. He recognized the limitation of His sphere and was faithful within it, and God raised up men through His labors; for it was Peter and John who ministered healing to the lame man at a later time. More needs will be met if our priority is to respond to His voice rather than to the needs themselves.

God has answers for those with needs who sincerely call on Him. However, His plan is often hindered by well-meaning saints who fail to see that God's *way* is best. By stepping into situations where God has not called us, we can hinder others He desires to use instead of us. Our time and energy are spent on something we are not called to do. Thus, our sphere is neglected and the work of another is hindered.

Equipping the saints involves training them how to *serve* in their spheres. Some leaders fail to allow those being trained to handle certain problems. Discipleship, or the training of leaders, should not maintain the candidates in a perpetual training mode. Discipleship is not an end. It is to be *a means* to the end. Those being trained must be given ever greater responsibility by which they can be tested and approved in their calling. This can be difficult if those overseeing the training are insecure. Fathers, however, will let their sons grow up. Growth may be painful and mistakes will be made. But God is raising up an army that will move in His power and His character. Ultimately, we shall see a people come forth who will do ever greater works to meet the needs of multitudes in this age.

2. *Local Church Structure:* The primary difference between an old wineskin and a new one is that the old one has become rigid, inflexible and unable to yield to the churning of new wine. New wine is a type of the Holy Spirit, and wineskins are a type of what contains the Spirit. Principally the wineskin represents one's heart. When our hearts are soft, tender and yielding to the Holy Spirit, we find that He comes and fills us with His presence. Hardness of heart guarantees His absence. Corporate church structures that are rigid, inflexible, etc., are not old wineskins. *They are symptoms of old wineskins!* When a group of people are continually filled with the Holy Spirit, their dependence is not on an organizational structure but on the life of God within them. God's life will lead them individually, under the oversight of men anointed to care for them. As each member finds his sphere of responsibility, the structure of the group will become apparent. Attempting to structure God's life is foolish. It is His life that structures us! May the joy of spontaneous obedience never be taken from His people by the constraints of men's interpretations of church order. Spontaneity is a vital part of church life and order.

Too often men do things because they are elders or home group leaders, etc., rather than because God has led them. It is so easy to fall into the rut of doing what others expect me to do because of having a title next to my name. At first glance it would seem a title is indeed a mark of being responsible. My question is, "responsible to what?" Are we to be responsible to a function, or to obey the Lord? Does the word "elder" define my task, or is it vice versa? It is as I give myself in obedience to the Lord in the task He has given me that the term "elder" makes sense. When men do God's will, others will recognize the grace that makes them elders, deacons, etc. The nature of apostolic ministry is no different. It is not that apostolic men structure the Church. Rather, they have grace to identify, point to, and lay hands on that which *Jesus is structuring through His life!* They are His fellow-workers (1 Cor. 3:9).

Jesus did not submit to structure; He submitted to His Father and thereby brought change to the structure! The Israel of God, as we see it in Acts 2, differed greatly from the Israel we see in the gospels. Out of the obedience of the Savior, the entire corporate face of the people of God was altered. That which emerged in the book of Acts was living, vital, full of the Spirit, etc. A new wineskin was formed! *Spontaneous obedience to the Lord Jesus is the only hope for ensuring that our local churches are moving in divine order.* Let each of us give ourselves wholeheartedly to the task Jesus has called us to.

When the saints come together for corporate worship, it is not to hear from men, but from God. Often men speak simply because others expect them to do so, not because God has given them something to say. In most fellowships there are a few from whom everyone expects to hear. However, the Lord wants to speak to His people and He has the right to speak through *any* saint He desires. Elders must oversee the meeting, but they must be careful not to "run" it. The days of a select few who "have the anointing" is over. Under the Old Covenant there was a separation between the priesthood and the "rest of Israel." Today, the Lord is raising up His body, a many-membered man, an *anointed, corporate priesthood.* Each member is being equipped for service.

The term "Christ" comes from the Greek word *"christos";* it means "anointed." Jesus was *the Anointed One;* He was *the Christ.* His body shares in that same anointing. The term "Body of Christ" (Body of the Anointed One) carries within its own wording this truth of the anointing. Our concepts and ministry must not hinder the emergence of the corporate, anointed man whom Jesus is raising up.

Unfortunately, there are times when, in our desire for order, we squelch those who have something valid to say from the Lord. Above all, Jesus must be heard! Leadership must know when to step back into the shadows. I do not have the right to speak because I am an elder; I only have the right if I have the word of the Lord in my mouth! Ordination does not guarantee everything I say will be anointed. We must be faithful *to Him,* not just to a position in the church.

I remember a particular meeting where the Lord taught me this truth. As different people shared, I heard a clear word being delivered to us. God was speaking to His people! Then someone said something that was theologically inaccurate. I looked to the Lord for His direction concerning the next step; He did not say a thing. It is situations like this that give leadership gray hairs! I could have stood up and spoken correction; after all, I was part of the eldership. However, I felt I was to be still. As I sat, waiting on Him, I sensed the Lord say that *if I spoke out of my position in the church, and not out of the anointing, I would create a greater problem. The life flow we had been experiencing would be further hindered by more words that were not anointed.* Then one of the brothers who has a prophetic call on his life stood and shared what he felt God was saying. As he spoke, it suddenly became clear what should take place. This brother had insight into what the Lord wanted to do. I sensed that God wished to introduce a teaching that one man in the fellowship had on his heart. Turning to this man I said, "Bruce, does this all fit with your message?"

"Don," he said, "my heart has been pounding so hard, I could hardly sit still." Sure enough, the Lord wanted him to speak and he went on to deliver a powerful remedial message from the heart of God.

When we speak in the congregation, we must contribute to the flow of God's river of life in our midst. The anointing releases rivers of living water from those who are led of the Spirit.

. . . *'From his innermost being shall flow rivers of living water.' (John 7:38)*

We all desire to hear God's voice more clearly while in His house. But this is not effected by just a few being released to speak. His voice is:

Like the sound of many waters. (Rev. 1:15)

Strength Is Weakness

Men and women who "know how to minister" in a professional sense always find it easy to go beyond what God gives them. This produces disorder. The humble, those who depend on His grace alone, will not make this mistake. Training for Christian ministry too often places an emphasis on *how to do* things rather than on building a dependency on the Lord. Thus, a proper foundation for ministry is not laid. Many valid ministers of the gospel are overly involved in church activity, overextended in their time and wondering where the joy of their salvation went. Human strength produces weakness. On the other hand, those who recognize their personal inability, will quickly sense the absence of His grace when they move beyond what the Lord has given them to do. Human strength (pride) helps perpetuate disorder. Seeing our own weakness (humility) helps establish God's order.

Our Response

Each individual organ in a physical body can be connected only to a certain number of other organs. In the same way, because of our limitations, the Lord has established a defined sphere of relationship for each of us in His body. A pastor can effectively relate to only a limited number of people. This is why biblical leadership in a local church consists of a plurality of men.

Each of us is responsible for recognizing the sphere God has given to us. We cannot sit back and ask others to define it for us. Overseers are to *confirm* and *adjust* what we believe God is saying to us, but they are not to take God's place in our lives. When we look to men for direction in an unhealthy way, the church soon begins to be organized rather than organic. This repeats the sin Israel committed when they said to Moses:

. . . *'Speak to us yourself and we will listen; but let not God speak to us, lest we die.' (Exod. 20:19)*

Israel rejected God's purpose for them. He wanted

them *all* to stand in His presence as a kingdom of priests. With human nature it is always easier to have others tell us what God is saying than to seek Him ourselves. Christendom has largely failed in the same way Israel did. We have not fully understood our call to be priests unto God.

We ought not function under the dictates of men. If we are involved in activities that do not have life, they should be laid down. To neglect our God-given stewardship and serve man is certain to bring frustration and leanness to our souls. True self-fulfillment is found in embracing the will of God.

Finally, the Church is to be apostolic, not because everybody in the local church is sent out apostolically, but because each one in the assembly finds his proper place. In this way, those who are called to travel will be released and sent out as a part of the local body.

. . . The whole body, being fitted and held together by that which every joint supplies, according to the proper working of each individual part, causes the growth of the body for the building up of itself in love. (Eph. 4:16)

A church that does not produce and release extra-local ministries is not a complete or mature assembly.

3

Tradition, Mixture and Moving On

"You say, 'We have a strong city; it cannot fail.' But I say to you, *'You have a strong tent; strong because of the well-sunken pegs. For that which I have given you as gifts to build you up and release my life within you, you have become dependent upon, and you are not dependent upon My life. But see, I am severing your ropes . . . .'* "

I could hardly believe my ears as I heard a brother prophesy these words one Sunday afternoon in our worship meeting. First of all, he was not even a committed member of our community. Yet the fact that God was speaking to us was obvious. What were we to do?

Our fellowship seemed to be doing so well! We had anointed worship, sound teaching, prophetic ministry, distribution of our teaching cassettes and tracts, home meetings, plurality of eldership, etc. And yet God was obviously not satisfied.

Up to this point I thought I had understood what transition was. But, as the next few years unfolded, the word "transition" began to take on new meaning.

Sure enough, God began to sever the ropes. The tent

had been tied to men and their ministries. God's intention for the ministries was that they should equip the people to lay hold of His life. Then the proper working of the individual members would cause the body to build itself up (Eph. 4:16). Somewhere along the line, we had failed in this. In one sense we elders had come between the people and God. They did not clearly see the need to seek the Lord in the Scriptures because of the teaching ministry in the pulpit. Excellent counseling was available, and some were finding more strength and security there than in Him. Emphasis was more on our need for each other than for Jesus.

Our desire to build a strong community was admirable, but the Master Architect had some adjustments to make among us. One by one those gift ministries that had been such a source of strength were revealed as weak in themselves. One elder went home to be with the Lord quite suddenly. Another had to pull back from ministry to focus his attention more on his family. A third was found with moral problems in his life. I also went through some personal shakings due to my desire for marriage (searching for a mate brings pain: embracing the will of God brings fulfillment!). While this was happening, I began to wonder if the church would survive! One day I sensed the Lord say to me, *"Son, whatever bears fruit, I prune that it may bear more fruit. You don't know what is coming in the future, but I do. In order for this fellowship to be prepared to stand and be fruitful in the midst of what is coming, I must take my pruning shears to it now." Present pruning is the key to future fruitfulness!*

Not only has the fellowship survived, but there has been increase! One would think that if the ropes to a tent were cut, it would fall. The miracle here was that this tent did not! We discovered that, we as an assembly, were not preserving His life; rather His life was preserving us! Our faith grew in Him and in what He was building. I am not so quick to say we have a "strong city" now, but I am,

Looking for the city which has foundations, whose architect and builder is God. (Heb. 11:10)

Apostolic Spheres

Turning our attention to the church in the New Testament, we see two quite different apostolic spheres of ministry. Apostles from Jerusalem labored among the Jews; Paul and those working with him served among the Gentiles. Unity existed between these groups; nevertheless, two distinct groups of churches did exist. An apostolic sphere is a number of churches related to a particular apostolic man or group of apostolic men. Paul planted many churches, including one at Corinth (2 Cor. 10:14; 1 Cor. 4:15); this church was part of Paul's apostolic sphere. Obviously Peter, Apollos and others had input there as well (1 Cor. 1:12), but Peter primarily labored among Jews and Paul among Gentiles (Gal. 2:7,9).

What is not obvious from the Scriptures is that one apostolic sphere was on the decline and one was on the upswing. The apostles from Jerusalem had a significant impact among Jewish people, and many were saved. However, the hand of God was increasingly upon the Gentile nations. It had always been His intention that *all* nations be touched by the light of His glory.

. . . I will build the Tabernacle of David . . . in order that the rest of mankind may seek the Lord, and all the Gentiles who are called by My Name." (Acts 15:16,17)

Speaking prophetically of the Lord Jesus, Isaiah says,

. . . It is too small a thing that you should be My Servant to raise up the tribes of Jacob and to restore the preserved ones of Israel; I will also make You a light of the nations so that My salvation may reach to the end of the earth. (Isa. 49:6)

The Scriptures refer to this present time as,

. . . The times of the Gentiles . . . (Luke 21:24)

Jesus had stated that the Temple would be destroyed. He declared that the glory had departed from it and that judgment was coming upon Jerusalem (Matt. 23:37,38; 24:2; Luke 21:20-24). He made it clear that His purpose involved more than "renewed Judaism." It was not the Gentiles' responsibility to become more Jewish in their life styles, rather the disciples were commanded to go to the nations and bring the good news of God's forgiveness to them. Yet over twenty years after the Lord's commission, multitudes of Jewish believers were still going to the Temple, worshiping and observing the Law (Acts 21:20). It appears something had "bogged down" in the apostolic sphere of the "Jerusalem brethren." They had not made the transition.

Our humanity is loath to let go of religious traditions even when God is no longer blessing them. As the Lord moves forward today in His purposes there is again a tendency toward *decline in apostolic purity* and *simplicity*. Often the desire to be "successful" can lead us into expedient practices. But that which "seems to work" and that which God is saying may not be the same thing. We *must* have a decrease of old priorities as God's new emphasis is revealed. This is true even if we are enjoying an increase in numbers of people, financial supply, ministerial polish, social acceptability and respectability, etc. Death comes from a decline of God's blessing.

Jesus apprehended Paul on the road to Damascus as part of His plan to evangelize the nations. From the beginning, Paul's ministry was distinct from what was happening in Jerusalem. Paul did submit his revelations to the men there because of their maturity and experience. But they contributed nothing new to what he had received (Gal. 2:2,6). Paul moved into the purposes of God without a significant contribution from Jerusalem. This was a healthy example for the leaders at Jerusalem; God's purpose is always bigger than our circle of influence!

The Pull of Tradition

The men at Jerusalem were imperfect, and so was Paul. The only *perfect* man who ever lived was Jesus Christ. *God used errant men to write inerrant Scriptures.* It is always a miracle when God uses men. Some believe Paul must have been almost perfect since God used him to write so much of the New Testament. However, Paul was flesh and blood just like the rest of us, and he made mistakes! We need to understand this, for if we do not, our tendency will be to believe a comparable apostolic ministry today is unattainable. When valid apostolic men do come across our paths, we will not receive them because they are "too human."

Timothy was an apostle (1 Thess. 1:1; 2:6), despite the fact that he was timid (2 Tim. 1:7), and had chronic physical ailments (1 Tim. 5:23). Also he did not appear confident in his calling and authority (1

Cor. 16:10). I wonder how many of us would receive a man such as Timothy as an apostle today.

It is not difficult to find weakness in Paul's life as well. Paul had purposed in his heart to return to the city of Jerusalem (Acts 19:21). Why did he wish to go? He wanted to be in Jerusalem to celebrate the Old Testament feast of Pentecost (Acts 20:16). However, this feast was fulfilled by the outpouring of the Holy Spirit recorded in Acts 2, just as Passover had been fulfilled at Calvary. God warned Paul, through a number of individuals, about what would happen to him if he went to Jerusalem.

. . . they kept telling Paul through the Spirit not to set foot in Jerusalem." (Acts 21:4)

Paul was told not to, but he was determined to go; he considered himself bound (Acts 20:22). He had purposed before God (Acts 19:21), and now he felt he must keep his "vow." Even God himself could not dissuade him. Jesus had said,

Make no oath at all, . . . but let your statement be, 'yes, yes' or 'no, no'; and anything beyond these is of evil. (Matt. 5:34,37)

There was evidence of bondage in Paul's heart.

The prophet Agabus warned Paul that if he went to Jerusalem the Jews would bind him (Acts 21:11). Luke and a number of disciples from Caesarea also pleaded with him to not go (Acts 21:12). Paul would not listen to their counsel. The only alternative for the brethren was to back away and trust God to care for His servant (Acts 21:14).

When Paul arrived in Jerusalem, he was received warmly. The leadership rejoiced at what God was doing through him among the Gentiles. However, their emphasis was pointing out what was happening among *them*.

You see, brother, how many thousands there are among the Jews of those who have believed, and they are all zealous for the Law; and they have been told about you, that you are teaching all the Jews who are among the Gentiles to forsake Moses, telling them not to circumcise their children nor walk according to the customs. What, then, is to be done? They will certainly hear that you have come. Therefore do this that we tell you. We have four men who are under a vow; Take them and purify yourself along with them, and pay their expenses in order that they may shave their heads; and all will know that there is nothing to the things which they have been told about you, but that you yourself also walk orderly, keeping the Law. (Acts 21:20-24)

James, a mighty man of God, was foremost in advising Paul to support the law. His counsel was a mixture of truth and old-covenant religion. The desire not to offend new Jewish believers, and "move in wisdom" was admirable. But truth was compromised! Paul, purified by the blood of Jesus (Heb. 1:3), was asked to purify himself *again*. He was to do this so he could enter a building devoid of God's glory (Matt. 23:38)! This action could only dishonor the Lord Jesus and His sacrifice at Calvary.

Then Paul took the men, and the next day purifying himself along with them, went into the temple, giving notice of the completion of the days of purification, until the sacrifice was offered for each one of them. (Acts 21:25)

Paul allowed a blood sacrifice to be offered up on his behalf! The perfect sacrifice for sin had already been offered once for all! Jesus had died to *remove* sins; animal sacrifices served only to *remind* people of their sins (Heb. 10:3). This counsel was clearly against the will of God. Jesus' blood was shed not only to wash away our sins, but also to cleanse our consciences from dead religious works, such as blood sacrifices (Heb. 9:14). God's people were to *put away* old-covenant ritual and embrace His righteousness through faith in Jesus.

When Paul participated in old-covenant ritual, he was being pulled by the tradition he had known since childhood. Religious tradition is a powerful thing to overcome. Paul had written many important truths contrasting justification by faith and living by the law. Yet we see him stumbling here. It is one thing to write and preach great truths; it is another to walk out fully what we preach. *Only Jesus did it perfectly.* This does not undermine the significant truths concerning justification by faith that Paul wrote in epistles prior to this event. It simply underscores his humanity. *Men,* inspired by God, wrote the Scriptures!

Why did God warn Paul so clearly and emphatically not to go back to Jerusalem? The answer lies in Agabus's prophecy:

The Jews at Jerusalem will bind the man who owns this belt . . . . (Acts 21:11)

It is interesting to note that the Jews did *not* bind Paul physically; the Romans chained him (Acts 21:33). Was Agabus's prophecy false? Did he make a mistake? No, God was not concerned about *physical* chains. The Lord could have destroyed any chains put upon His servant. Physical imprisonment was simply not the Lord's concern. He was indicating that if Paul went back to Jerusalem, he would find pressure from his Jewish brethren to step back into bondage of the law he had been delivered from. There would be a binding of Paul's *spirit* through men who were still caught up in old-covenant ritual. If, in fact, Agabus was referring to *physical* bondage, then he was wrong in his prophecy for it was the Romans who chained Paul. If he was prophesying of *spiritual* bondage, then we must conclude that God did not want Paul in Jerusalem. God never wants His people in spiritual bondage!

It is also interesting to note that Agabus bound his *own* feet and hands. The binding would happen in that manner. The implication here is that Paul was bringing this bondage *upon himself.* It was not something God wanted him to experience. It was something he would reap because of the pull of tradition in his human nature to the law.

Some have said that Paul allowed animals to be sacrificed on his behalf that he might be as one under the law in order to win those under the law (1 Cor. 9:20). Thus, this was permissible behavior by Paul and illustrated how we are to:

> Become all things to all men . . . . (1 Cor. 9:22)

in order to see them saved.

My response is this. Ask yourself, "Would I allow someone to sacrifice an animal so they could then receive me as righteous when my message to them is that I am already righteous because of Calvary?" That does not make sense. It undermines the gospel message! Righteousness is not attained through the shedding of animal blood. Those who do so should be confronted, not agreed with! Truth will set them free. The temptation is to accommodate mixture for that may make us popular, but it does not help others in their relationship to God.

A Lesson Learned

It is helpful for us to see Paul's humanity. In many respects he was just like the rest of us. Like us, he also reaped the results of his mistake. He was imprisoned. However, the gospel he continued to minister was not hindered. It continued to spread with great power. God's Word can not be chained.

Paul's letters from prison reveal that he gained valuable insight through this whole series of events. For example, consider his epistle to Colossae.

See to it that no one takes you captive through philosophy and empty deception according to the tradition of men . . . . (Col. 2:8)

He goes on to say that salvation is found only in the person of the Lord Jesus Christ. Fulfillment is found in Him (Col. 2:9,10). True circumcision occurs when we are baptized into Him (Col. 2:10,11). His death on Calvary brought us forgiveness and a total cancellation of the "legal debts" that we piled up because of our sin against God (Col. 2:13,14).

Therefore let no one act as your judge in regard to food or drink or in respect to a festival or a new moon or a Sabbath day—things which are a mere shadow of what is to come; but the substance belongs to Christ. (Col. 2:16,17)

Obviously something was indelibly written upon Paul's heart after his return to Jerusalem and subsequent imprisonment.

Seeds of Pride Evident At Jerusalem?

Was the church at Jerusalem the pattern for building God's house? The answer is no, for basic deficiencies existed there.

One of the first signs of spiritual decline in any church is pride. The statement, "look at the tremendous things God is doing" becomes, "look at the tremendous things God is doing *among us*." In the beginning stages of a revival, people are caught up with the awesome presence of God. Nothing else matters. Pride is not evident. Any manifestation of it would be quickly recognized in such an atmosphere.

Eventually, however, something must be built. Life always has structure to it. Even as the life of a tree produces an intricately structured leaf, so also God's life produces structure among His people. Problems arise, however, when our attention becomes focused more on the structure than on God whose life and presence produced it. Leaders soon face structure upkeep and repair. Administration of what has been built becomes the order of the day. Very often men who once moved under an anointing become increasingly involved in administrative tasks to keep "the work" going. The prophetic thrust is then blunted. Instead of declaring what God *is building,* the primary emphasis is on maintaining what *has been built.*

At this point there are two options that confront the builder in God's house:

1. Settle in and give himself to maintaining the structure.
2. Humble himself and cry out to God for fresh insight concerning what to do. The Lord might very well respond like this, *"Take your hands off what has been built. Whatever is held up by your efforts I want to fall to the ground. Whatever is held up by Me will never fall!"* As hard as this is for a builder to hear, this is a great truth! God wants to

keep us from building, "wood, hay and stubble" on the foundation of the Lord Jesus.

What is the root of our turmoil and struggle when God asks us to let go of something? Is it not that our identity is in that which has been built, rather than in the Lord? Why does a sense of security come from seeing what has emerged through our ministry? Part of the answer is *pride*. From this root comes a fear that we will be seen as a failure if what we have labored over should tumble to the ground. But it is precisely what *does* fall that *is* our "wood, hay and straw." Conversely, what does not fall is our, "gold, silver and precious stones." How much better to discover *today* what is "wood, hay and straw" than to have it revealed at Jesus' second coming! This is the mercy of God.

The Church is held together either by the power of God, or by organization. If the latter, then the burden lies on our shoulders. If it is His responsibility, we are then released to obey Him and leave the consequences in His hands. Humbling ourselves enables us to move on with God. Pride prevents us from doing so.

In the church at Jerusalem, it appears that an element of pride or elitism was present in the leadership. Consider their counsel to Paul.

Purify yourself . . . , and pay their expenses; and all will know that there is nothing to the things which they have been told about you, but that you yourself also walk orderly, keeping the law. But concerning the Gentiles who have believed, we wrote, having decided that they should abstain from meat sacrificed to idols and from blood and from what is strangled and from fornication. (Acts 21:24,25)

The implication from their counsel is this: "It is fine for Gentiles to follow only these four requirements and not the whole law, but Paul *you are a Jew!* God expects more from you." Such thinking would indicate a "two-class" concept of people in the Kingdom. One class would consist of Jews, the other of Gentiles. Jews would be required to have a different life style than Gentiles. This was precisely the bondage that Paul was drawn into. (See also Gal. 2:11-13)

In Acts 15, the apostles and elders concluded that Gentile believers did not have to be circumcised to be saved; this was meant to set them free from the requirements of the Law. While it did have this effect on the Gentiles, yet the decision implied an opposite direction for the Jews; they would still be circumcised. Instead of seeing that *no one* should live by the law, they concluded that *some* did not have to. Thus a "two-class" concept of believers existed.

Let us never hold so tightly to what God *has* blessed, that we fail to move on in what He *is* doing. To do so brings a mixture, it is always God's perfect will for us to move on!

The Unhealthy Elevation of Men

Men from Jerusalem's apostolic sphere came to the Galatian churches and taught them that salvation was found through faith in Christ *plus* keeping the law. This was a clear distortion of the gospel (Gal. 1:7). These men also attacked Paul's character, referring to him as a man-pleaser. We see Paul's defense in Galatians 1:10:

For am I now seeking the favor of men, or of God? Or am I striving to please men? If I were still trying to please men, I would not be a bond servant of Christ.

The word "still" indicated that when deeply involved in Jewish religion Paul was a man pleaser. Now he is concerned with pleasing God. The implication is that those attacking him and preaching a mixture of grace and law were the real "man pleasers." Those who mix the pure Word of God with the traditions of men are generally very concerned with what others think of them.

The fear of man brings a snare . . . . (Prov. 29:25)

These teachers were snaring others into bondage and were ensnared themselves.

Paul's response was to point out that his gospel did not originate from other men.

The gospel which was preached by me is not according to man. For I neither received it from man, nor was I taught it, but I received it through a revelation of Jesus Christ." (Gal. 1:11,12)

The gospel can set men free, because it does not originate in men nor is it dependent on the approval of men. Whether men reject or receive it, God's truth remains unchanged. But to the degree there is mixture, there will be a loss of freedom. God's truth has come to set us free (Gal. 5:11). However, to be free we must accept persecution for the cross of Christ. These false teachers would not do so.

Those who desire to make a good showing in the flesh try to compel you to be circumcised, simply that they may not be persecuted for the cross of Christ. (Gal. 6:12)

What we have seen so far in this section can be summed up in this formula:

The fear of man → mixture → loss of freedom.
God speaks truth → men receive the pure gospel → find freedom.

One result of fearing man is to develop an unhealthy elevation of leaders. The teachers of mixture who came among the Galatians probably had this attitude toward the apostles in Jerusalem. In his letter, Paul takes time to underscore the humanity of those apostles. Why did he do this? Obviously, he was endeavoring to undo something that had been imparted to the Galatians. Paul was not maliciously exposing sin but underscoring their humanity as he "brought them down a few notches" in the eyes of the Galatians.

But from those who were of high reputation (what they were makes no difference to me; God shows no partiality)—well, those who were of reputation contributed nothing to me. (Gal. 2:6)

The men of reputation here included Peter, James, and John (Gal. 2:7-9).

Paul also recounts an incident where Peter stumbled much like the Galatians were now doing (Gal. 2:11-14).

When men are elevated in an unhealthy way, God will see to it that they are brought down a few notches in our eyes. This is a fearful thing. However it is a safeguard both for the church and for those in leadership. It is easy to allow others to view us as being greater than we really are.

The Opportunity To Move On

It is not clear whether these teachers of mixture among the Galatians came from Jerusalem or not. However, they were obviously from the apostolic sphere that the men from Jerusalem labored in. I doubt that Peter, James and John had a close relationship with these men, but it appears that they did tolerate them. Indeed they permitted what Paul would not.

We see an example of this in Acts 15 when men came to Antioch from Judea and preached that Gentiles had to be circumcised to be saved. Paul and Barnabas had great dissension and debate with them. Why had James not responded like Paul? Probably because he and the other apostolic men in Jerusalem had been teaching or at least tolerating them. While not specifically giving them instruction to teach these things, they did admit that these men had come from their midst (Acts 15:24).

The leadership in Jerusalem had not been clear in its preaching of the gospel. As a consequence, men were emerging in ministry who believed a mixture of grace and law. God wanted this issue dealt with, and He used Paul to bring it to the surface. The results of the council in Acts 15 were questionable. They concluded that *Gentiles* did not have to be circumcised to be saved. However, God's heart was that *no one* had to be circumcised to be saved. I believe the record of Acts 15 reveals the point in time where God gave the church of Jerusalem the option to take a clear stand and move on in Him. It appears they did not do so. Their conclusion as reflected in their edict was a mixture. Decline began to set in.

When we tolerate what God would have us adjust, the result can only be mixture in how we build.

Is Being Apostolic Enough?

The church at Jerusalem was apostolic. The community there was an example of Christian character in many ways. They loved one another enough to sell their possessions when needs arose (Acts 2:45; 4:34,35). They released men to travel and preach the gospel. They loved the Lord Jesus and rejoiced at what He was doing among the Gentiles. Yet there was mixture in how they built. It is not enough to be apostolic; we must be *faithful in following* the Lord Jesus. Just because a church is apostolic does not mean it is built correctly. There are wise builders and there are unwise builders. Calling is not synonymous with success. Just because one is called to be an apostle does not mean he will function as he ought to.

The charismatic renewal has been a mighty visitation from the Lord. Apostolic and prophetic men have emerged. Different apostolic circles now dot the spiritual countryside. We stand at the beginning of a new visitation; and it is a time to make choices. When Jesus speaks we must move on. Winds of change are blowing; it is a time of transition.

The temptation will be to maintain and renew what was built in the seventies. Many beautiful truths were restored to the Church through the charismatic renewal. We learned about relationship, discipleship, shepherding, community, family order, etc. We have built with these truths. The danger is that it is easy to find our identity in these things more than in Christ. God's people need to hear fresh things from the heart of the Lord, not "the party platform."

Clearly some of what we have built will need adjustment. We do not hear perfectly; therefore, what we have built is not exact. Our God, however, is a precision builder, and He requires that we build accurately in this hour. Let us maintain teachable hearts and make the adjustments that He requires.

Conclusion

God is doing great and mighty things in our day. What a privilege it is to know Him and to behold the unfolding transitions of His plan. Central to His purpose is the revelation of His Son. Today, Jesus is being revealed in greater measure within the Church. Finally, He is going to be revealed in all His majesty to the whole earth when He returns. Our number-one priority is to know Him intimately for this is the essence of eternal life (John 17:3). As we walk with Him, we must be faithful to Him, not just to tasks He has given us to perform. We must live and move in His life, not stagnate in maintenance activity of "structural upkeep."

Each of us has a unique sphere of responsibility in His body. It is vital that we find this place of service and walk faithfully with Him in it. Our sphere will be defined by His life, not the needs of men or the "general good" of some church structure. Dependence upon Him will bring both individual clarity to us and order to His Church.

As there was with Paul, there will be temptations back to religious tradition we have been delivered from. Pride, the fear of man, and the unhealthy elevation of leaders are some of the pitfalls that keep us from God's best. However, as we focus the eyes of our hearts upon Jesus, we will find these snares and other strategies of the enemy to be places of victory and occasions for God to glorify His Name in us. We are in transition, becoming the people upon whom His glory will arise in the days of darkness ahead.

When all is said and done, to do His will brings the greatest joy and sense of fulfillment to His people; He knows the longings of our hearts better than we do. As we walk in obedience with Him, we will find many surprises awaiting us. As we maintain teachable and humble hearts, we can make the necessary transitions into new dimensions of His purposes.

PREPARED FOR HIS Glory

Dale Rumble

WHAT IS IT THAT PREPARES A MAN FOR GOD'S GLORY. IN THIS BOOK, DALE RUMBLE CHALLENGES YOUR HEART TO RESPOND TO THE SPIRIT OF THE LORD TO BE FOUNDED IN THE FAITH OF THE LORD JESUS CHRIST.

AVAILABLE AT CHRISTIAN BOOKSTORES EVERYWHERE.